First Time Homebuyer *Gold*

J. BAPTISTE

First Time Homebuyer Gold

Visit our website at www.StillwaterPress.com for more information.

First Stillwater River Publications Edition

ISBN: 978-1-958217-99-3

1 2 3 4 5 6 7 8 9 10

Written by J. Baptiste.
Cover & interior book design by Matthew St. Jean.
Published by Stillwater River Publications, Pawtucket, RI, USA.

Names: Baptiste, J. (Joycelyn), author.
Title: First time homebuyer gold / J. Baptiste.
Description: First Stillwater River Publications edition. | Pawtucket, RI, USA : Stillwater River Publications, [2023]
Identifiers: ISBN: 978-1-958217-99-3
Subjects: LCSH: House buying--United States. | Real property--Purchasing--United States. | Home ownership--United States. | Finance, Personal.
Classification: LCC: HD1375 .B36 2023 | DDC: 643.12--dc23

This book is dedicated to . . .

My true love God Almighty for helping me to discover and share with the world the purpose you have created within me. Also, for those relentless cupid arrows of love, discipline, obedience, focus, and motivation.

Far beyond any limits of the sky . . .

&

Gregory J. Schadone, Esq. and Jamie Gau, thank you so much for all of your assistance with this project!

&

Elizabeth E. Beaudry, for reminding me constantly to buy a comma and for selflessly sacrificing time for our many reads. Thank you!

Contents

Purchasing?	1
Research	2
Where Do You Want to Reside?	4
Your Offer	6
Fixed or Adjustable-Rate Mortgage?	7
Earnest Money/Good Faith Deposit	8
The Process	9
Purchase and Sale	11
The Process II	12
Documents	15
First-Time Home Buyer Education Course	16
Extenuating Factors	17
Employment	18
Debt Calculations	20
Assets and Large Deposits	24
Gift Letters	26
Down Payment	27
Down Payment Assistance	29
Lender Credit	30
Rates	31

Escrow 32
Credit Report/FICO 34
Fixing My Credit 36
Credit History 38
Say What? 40
Fixer-Upper vs. Drop Bags Home 42
Home Appraisal 43
Home Inspections 46
Land 48
Property Boundaries 50
Oil Tank 52
Cesspool/Septic 53
Flood Insurance 54
Homeowner's Insurance 56
Initial/Final Walk-Through 59
After Closing 61
Best Wishes! 63

About the Author 65

Purchasing?

Welcome! It is awesome that you have decided to take that step in purchasing your first home. The process may seem a little bit overwhelming, which is especially true if you do not have any mortgage experience and are new to this journey. This book will help to simplify things for you, so be sure to read it to its entirety. One key tip I can provide to you is: always live within your means and budget. It is okay to say no if a situation does not work, fit your needs, or provide you with any benefit. Stand your ground if you feel firm in a particular matter (try to negotiate) while avoiding bidding wars (unless you decide you absolutely love and must purchase the home or property). This book is designed to give you a simple yet very detailed understanding of the mortgage process. As a first-time homeowner, you may be eligible (as applicable) for tax breaks, deductions, and other benefits, which may come in handy. Eager to learn more? Let's begin!

Research

Let's take a few moments to quickly analyze your overall picture prior to beginning your journey.

- First, what are your objectives and goals regarding purchasing your new home?
- Have you researched and understood both the pros and cons of purchasing a home verses renting one?
- Are there any foreseeable barriers or impediments that could stop you from purchasing the home of your dreams?
- Have you determined where you would like to reside (city, urban, rural, or suburban)?
- Are you aware of what factors to look out for when purchasing your first home?
- What is your purchasing limit?
- Have you decided which company you will use as your lender to obtain your mortgage?
- How high are you willing to offer above your purchasing limit?

- What type of home are you looking to purchase (single family, condo, etc.)?
- Have you analyzed your finances?
- Have you decided who will complete your home inspections, title work, etc.?
- Have you decided which closing attorney you would like to use?
- You can also select the title company of your choice or waive this option.

Research and select a title attorney to handle your documents. In some states, a buyer is required to have an attorney present during closing (check to see if your state is one of those states). These questions may seem a little overbearing, but knowing the answers prior to reading this book will help to strengthen your thought process along the way.

Where Do You Want to Reside?

When looking for a home, your realtor can provide you with homes applicable to the search criteria you provide them. You can also search online and look up homes that fit your criteria for the area you are looking to reside. Realtor.com, Zillow.com, or other search engines can provide you with listings of homes that are available for sale. It is important to stay active on the listings and advise your realtor (if they don't contact you first) if you see a property you are interested in. Most homes listed for sale go under contract/pending rather quickly. Realtor.com can provide you with tools to search for a realtor (if one is needed).

When deciding where you would like to purchase a home and reside, there are some factors (as applicable to your area) that you should keep in mind. They may or may not affect your purchasing decision. These factors below are in regard to how close in proximity they are to the home you are purchasing. You should look out for the following:

- landfill/hazardous waste landfill
- wastewater/sewer treatment facility
- swamps/marshes

- nuclear power plant
- railroad/train station
- airport
- trash collection sites
- waste transfer station
- oil refineries
- rail yards
- natural gas power plants

Once you have confirmed your potential new home, sites like Zillow or other online searches can provide you with the crime data for the area. You can also drive by the area to obtain a feel for the location. The tax assessor's website for the address of the home you are purchasing may be able to provide you with tax information. It may reflect if the taxes increased, remained somewhat constant, or decreased each year. You can locate the county of the home you are purchasing from the purchase and sale agreement or other source. Once you have the county, you can look up the assessor for the specific county either online or by telephone.

If purchasing a condo, look for the amount of the homeowners' association (HOA) fees and inquire to your realtor as to what they cover (water, sewer, heat, landscaping, trash removal, etc.). Having HOA fees that cover water and sewer are great but only if the fee is on the low side. Be sure to read in their entirety the condo declarations. This outlines all of the rules, regulations, etc. of the association. Even if you are not purchasing a condo, check to see if the house of your choice is in an HOA. Even some single unit detached homes can be in an HOA, so be sure to double check with your agent.

Your Offer

Research online and confirm at the tax assessor's website (if one is available) to see how much the seller paid for the home. The home and the asking price should be in conjunction with one another.

Ex: If the home is being sold for $200,000 and the comps (similar homes) were sold for $180,000, confirm to see if the seller has completed any improvements to support the $200,000 asking price. You need to be sure that when you make an offer, it is a solid one but within your means. Do your research.

Fixed or Adjustable-Rate Mortgage?

What is the price range you have decided on for your new home ($150,000, $200,000, etc.)? This is key to note, for you will have to factor in the monthly payment into your monthly debt amount. An online search for a mortgage calculator can provide you with an approximation of how much the payments may be. You can also contact your lender of choice and inquire about current rates and terms. The terms are how long you would like to payback your mortgage (fifteen years, thirty years, adjustable rate, etc.). Would you like to have a fixed-rate mortgage (payments remain the same each month) or would you like an adjustable-rate mortgage where the payments adjust (increase) at certain set times? Adjustable-rate mortgages often have lower initial starting rates than fixed-rate mortgages. However, be sure to understand when and by how much your payment could increase.

Ex: With an adjustable-rate mortgage your initial payment could be $550. As the mortgage adjusts, it could increase to $900. As the mortgage continues to adjust, your payment will continue to increase. Be sure you can afford the payments if this is the right option for you.

Earnest Money/Good Faith Deposit

When you have found a home, the seller has accepted your offer, and you have signed the purchase and sale agreement, you will most likely have to provide an earnest money/ good faith deposit. This is a sum of money, either a certain percentage of the purchase price or an agreed upon sum of money between you and the seller, that is put down to demonstrate your seriousness in purchasing the home. Sometimes the earnest money deposit can be added to the buyer's down payment or closing costs. You will pay the earnest money/good faith deposit to an escrow account or trust (held under a title company, real estate broker, law firm, etc.). The funds will remain there until the loan closes or some other unforeseen factor occurs (breach of contract, significant defects in the home, if a buyer is denied financing, etc.). You will need to read your purchase and sale agreement carefully and be sure you understand the conditions of refunding the earnest money/good faith deposit. Also, be sure you are aware (as reflected in your purchase and sale agreement) of the applicable factors where you can lose your earnest money/ good faith deposit. If there is anything you do not understand, please check with your realtor and/or lender for clarification.

The Process

A lender usually pulls the credit of the individual attempting to purchase a home and reviews it. Depending on certain factors, the lender will issue a pre-approval or pre-qualification letter reflecting certain terms (loan amount, program, etc.). Please note that you do not need a pre-approval letter to view a home for sale, but it is great to have when planning to make an offer on the home. It is usually requested by the seller's realtor when an offer is about to be made on the home. It confirms that the loan amount you are pre-approved for is sufficient enough to cover the asking price of the seller. Be sure to check your pre-approval letter for an expiration date and inquire to your lender about the details. If it expires and you have not yet found a home, you can request an extension. When you have decided to make an offer on the home, your realtor will draft either an offer letter or an offer to purchase letter depending on how you would like to submit your offer. If you decide to submit the offer letter, it will reflect the purchase price of your choosing, estimated closing date, terms, and other contingent factors which will need to be met. It advises the seller that you are interested in the home and would like to place an offer on it. Once the offer letter has been provided to the seller's realtor, it will then be given to the seller for review. Once the seller has reviewed the document, they can either counteroffer (return with another offer terms, different from the ones you initially provided), accept your initial offer, or fully decline your offer. If you decide to have your offer submitted using the offer to purchase letter, it advises the seller that you are truly serious about the home and would like to submit an offer to *purchase* the home. The offer to purchase reflects the proposed terms and conditions between you, the buyer, and the seller in a real estate transaction. Once you and the seller have read the document, reviewed it with your agent and/or attorney, and agreed to its contents, you will need to sign and date it confirming such. Once this happens, the document becomes a legally binding agreement.

Purchase and Sale

The purchase and sale agreement is the legally binding agreement between you (the buyer) and the seller. Be sure to read this document to its entirety and question anything that you don't understand. Although your agent will play a central role in this stage, you have the right to have an attorney review, negotiate, edit, and explain the contract before you sign. The purchase and sale agreement is the most important document in this process as it outlines the terms and conditions, purchase price, and other important factors. This agreement between you and the seller, once signed and dated by both parties and all other parties involved, is fully binding. The purchase and sale agreement will also provide for any contingences that will protect you moving forward. You want to make sure everything you understood and agreed to previously is contained within the purchase and sale agreement. The purchase and sale agreement will contain very important and time sensitive dates. These dates can include delivery of the earnest money deposit, property inspections, appraisal date, mortgage contingency date, and the closing date. It is imperative that you pay attention to them and be sure you adhere to them. Remember to be strong and take the reins of your purchase with confidence.

The Process II

Once the purchase and sale agreement has been fully executed, signed, and dated by you and the seller, a copy of the document will be provided to your lender. This allows your lender to connect with the closing attorney and begin the title work. During the processing of your loan, your lender will request specific documentation from you in order to proceed with your loan review (identification, income, assets, etc.). Be sure you obtain the name and contact information of those you are working with (i.e., loan officer, processor, loan officer assistant, etc.). In the meantime, you are responsible for selecting the company you would like to have complete the inspections on the home you are purchasing. It is your responsibility to have the inspections scheduled, paid for upfront, and completed on the property. Remember you are not able to select who completes the appraisal on your home, but you will be required to pay for the appraisal either upfront or at the closing. You will also be responsible for contacting a carrier of homeowner's insurance and flood insurance (if needed) to insure your home. The lender will also assign an underwriter to review the documentation you provided, along with your credit, income, and assets to the loan program that is a best fit for your profile. It is best to have all of the necessary documents readily available and organized. Remember, as the process proceeds, more documentation may be requested from you. Be sure to provide the lender with the homeowner's insurance and flood insurance (if needed) documentation. The loan officer will stay abreast to confirm that once the appraisal is completed, the value of the home is sufficient (supports the asking price of the seller).

Ex: Your loan amount is $150,000. The appraisal has been completed and the property value is $140,000. With the appraisal coming in at a lower value, the lender will have to rework your loan due to the lower value. On the other side, if the appraisal came in higher, for example $160,000, your loan amount would be supported for there is sufficient value in the home.

Other factors will also be taken into consideration with the review of your loan process, including any issues with the inspections, defects in the home, issues noted on the appraisal, etc. Once the underwriter completes the review on your loan file, they will refer it for either an approval, further review and request more documentation/clarification, or denial. If your loan is approved, the attorney has confirmed the title is clear and marketable, and all conditions and stipulations have been met, you will receive a clear to close. A clear to close is simply that all of the factors have been met and you are clear to close. This is the go ahead for the title company to schedule your closing and draft closing documents. Remember, just because you are clear to close, this does not mean that you can now proceed to open new credit, for it may cause you to potentially be denied. Remember, your credit is checked prior to the closing on your loan and any new debt reflecting may be taken into consideration. Confirm that you, the lender, your realtor, and the closing attorney/title company are on the same page when it comes to the closing date. Be sure to perform your final walk-through of the property on the same day of closing (if possible). On your closing day, ownership will be transferred from the seller to you (the buyer). The deed to the property will be updated and recorded to reflect your name. Be sure to double check all of the documentation you are signing for accuracy, including the closing disclosure (CD), loan application, and good faith estimate (GFE). Let us look a little deeper into the process before I bid you welcome home.

Documents

During the entire process of the loan, be sure to review all of the documents that are provided to you. Carefully check the spelling of your full name, date of birth, social security number, address, employer, phone numbers, and other information. If there is something wrong or some form of discrepancy on one or more of the documents, bring it to the attention of the lender immediately. If your mailing address is separate from the address that you are purchasing, be sure to bring this to the attention of the lender.

Ex: Your mailing address is a post office box and the residence address you are purchasing will be only your physical address. Do not depend on the lender or financial institution to confirm all information on your documents are correct. Remember, mistakes do happen. Also, check your appraisal, completed property inspections (if any), note, mortgage, application, and all documents for accuracy.

Be sure to confirm that any fees you are paying as applicable (appraisal, home inspection, etc.) are reflected on the correct side of the closing disclosure, or CD, depending on who is responsible for them (buyer or seller). They would be listed on the buyer side of the CD only if you are paying for those fees.

First-Time Home Buyer Education Course

As a first-time homebuyer, you will be required to take an education course (in most states). The course usually explains and breaks down what will be expected of you as a buyer. It also gives you a chance to understand, firsthand, most of the factors in purchasing a home. In most states, the first-time education course is free of charge, so be sure to inquire in your specific state (for a fee maybe required). Once you complete the course, you will be provided with a certificate. This certificate will advise the lender that you have completed the required education course. It is a good idea to ask any questions that you may have during your class session. Anything that is unclear, inquire to your lender and/or realtor.

Extenuating Factors

Once you are under contract in your purchasing journey, be sure you are aware of any and all important factors. Be sure to keep all of your payments on your liabilities (debt) current and try not to miss making any payments. If there is an extenuating circumstance (emergency, surgery, sudden care of a family member, etc.), it is imperative to make note as to when it started, what occurred, how long you missed payments, and when you plan to bring the account(s) current (if possible). Your lender will inquire if this affected your credit and employment (leave of absence, new job, gaps in employment, etc.). When advising your lender, try to be as accurate with the information as you can.

Employment

For income documentation, have on hand two years of income, either W-2's or, if paid differently, two forms of your tax filing pay document received from your employer or self-employment.

Keep at least one month of paystubs.

Ex: If applying for a mortgage in April, provide a month's worth of paystubs for March (or as your lender instructs), and as the process progresses, your lender may request April paystubs. If needed, maintain copies of your filed tax returns. The lender will be able to obtain this information on their own; however, they may ask you for a copy of the last two or three years (as applicable) filed and match those to the actual records they receive from verifying your returns filed with the IRS, so it is imperative your numbers are accurate.

Another factor is to avoid changing jobs (if you can) during your mortgage process. Most lenders (as applicable) would require a two-year employment history and would want to be sure you are stable with your employer. If you absolutely have to change jobs during your mortgage process, confirm that it is a positive shift.

Example:

Old position: Your previous job position was hourly, and you were earning $18.00 per hour, thirty hours a week.

New position: Your new career (job position) is now salary earning $55,000 annually working forty hours a week.

The new career (job change) is a positive shift because you will be earning more income and working more hours.

Debt Calculations

During your mortgage process, if you have credit cards, do not (if possible) make any expensive purchases on them. Continue to make your payments on your existing debt and keep your accounts current. Depending on what route you would like to take, most loan programs have a max debt-to-income (DTI) ratio that they use, so it is important not to open new debt during the mortgage process. This can affect your chances of qualifying for a home. If you are wondering how this is even possible, keep reading. The lender will use a calculation called the debt-to-income ratio or DTI ratio. This calculation takes your total monthly debt payments and divides that amount by your monthly gross income.

*For this example, your loan program *max* DTI is 50 percent.

Ex: Your *only* monthly creditors and monthly payments are:

- $224.00 monthly payment to credit card company A
- $96.00 monthly payment to auto loan company Z
- $199.00 monthly payment to credit card company B

When you add all of the total monthly payments it equals $519.00 (debt). Your monthly gross income is $3,000.

Now let's determine your DTI.

<u>Monthly debt payments total $519.00</u>
Monthly gross income is $3,000 = debt-to-income (DTI) ratio is 17.3 percent

Using this example, the DTI is very low at 17 percent, which is great. There are no issues, and you were *initially* approved for your loan because the DTI is within standards and under 50 percent. Congrats!

Now let's look at the flip side as to what can happen and potentially disqualify you. Remember the lender will pull your credit report again during the mortgage qualifying process, so if new debt appears on your credit report (depending on the amount of the debt), you may no longer qualify for your loan.

*We will continue to use the loan program *max* DTI of 50 percent.

Ex: You decided that since you are already *initially* approved with a 17.3 percent DTI, you were all set. You take the opportunity to purchase various items that you want and can use in your new home.

- Your first purchase is a $2,000 furniture set (monthly payment of $175.00) from store H which will look great in your new home.

- Also, you decided to treat yourself and purchased an $80,000 automobile (monthly payment $1,200) on auto loan X.

Your lender pulls your credit report again and notices the new debts that you incurred. In adding these new debts, your DTI will change. The lender will now reevaluate your situation and determine if you still qualify.

Let's rework the numbers.

Your monthly debts and monthly payments are now:

- $224.00 monthly payment to credit card company A
- $96.00 monthly payment to auto loan company Z
- $199.00 monthly payment to credit card company B
- $175.00 monthly payment to furniture store company H
- $1,200 monthly payment to auto loan company X

When you add all of the total monthly payments it equals $1,894 (debt). There were no changes in your monthly gross income of $3,000.

Now let's determine your DTI.

<u>Monthly debt payments total $1,894</u>
Monthly gross income is $3,000 = debt-to-income (DTI) ratio is 63.1 percent

Using this example, the DTI is very high at 63.1 percent and over the loan program max of 50 percent. With the increase in DTI, you currently do not qualify for the loan program. The lender will have to work with you to assist you in either finding a new loan program, encourage you to pay down/off some of the incurred debt, or may need to deny your loan based on the new DTI.

It is easy to see how quickly you can go from being qualified to denied. It is imperative during the mortgage process not to open any new debts. Remember, late payments affect your credit which in turn affects your credit score and credit profile (from "on-time payments" to "late," "delinquent," etc.).

Remember, this is just an example so that you obtain a better understanding as to how the debt-to-income ratio is calculated. Everyone has different factors in their situation, and all are unique.

Assets and Large Deposits

You may hear the term *source* when it relates to the assets you will be using in accordance with your loan. Let's break it down a little further. *Source* means where the funds are being held. A lender needs to be able to receive true, accurate, and legible documentation from either a financial or investment company reflecting the current amount of funds you have maintained to use for your loan. While it may be tempting to keep the funds that you will be using in your mortgage process under the mattress, hidden within a picture frame, tucked away somewhere else in your home, or any other unsourced area, this is not a good idea. Your lender will require statements, which are either from a 401(k) account, checking account, savings account, gift funds (someone is providing you with the funds to help you with the loan), etc. Be sure you are able to obtain and provide at least two months of statements to your lender.

Ex: You are under contract on April first. Your lender may require you to provide statements for the account you are using for your assets to pay for closing costs and down payment (as applicable) for the months of March and February. As the mortgage process continues, you will also need to provide another statement prior to your closing to confirm that you still have the necessary funds. Remember, the statements will need to be for the accounts you will be using funds from to pay your down payment and/or closing costs (as applicable).

If you are using funds (assets) in accordance with your mortgage process, try not to make any large deposits to it (if possible). Large deposits are sometimes considered a flag to the lender, and they will require you to explain in writing the reason for the large deposit and/or provide additional documentation if needed. The additional documentation will most likely be in the form of statements from either a financial institution or investment company.

Ex: You are using funds from your checking account with bank S in your mortgage process. You provided your lender with two months' copies of your bank statements. While reviewing your checking account statement, your lender notices that you made two $50,000 deposits to your checking account on different dates. Your lender may request documentation that confirms where the $50,000 deposits originated. The request for additional documentation may apply depending on any other large deposits noted or other factors (as applicable to your situation).

Gift Letters

In the event that you need help with paying your down payment, obtaining a gift letter may be a possible option. A gift letter is a legal document from an eligible donor (a family member, friend, etc.) offering funds to the buyer as a gift. The donor may pay the down payment in full or in part, but it must be documented. Some programs allow the buyer to gift the entire down payment (check with your lender). Be sure that whoever is providing you with the necessary funds is advised that the funds are a gift and not a loan. The donor is not allowed to provide you with funds that they would consider to be paid back on loan at a later date; it must be a gift. Please note that the donor who will be providing you the gift funds will have to source where the funds are being held. Remember, the source is where the funds are coming from (checking account, savings account, 401(k), etc.).

Ex: If the donor signs the letter advising that they are gifting $5,000 from their checking account at bank Y, then they must provide proof that they have the necessary funds with a checking account bank statement. This is done not only to confirm proof of funds, but to also protect you in case the funds are not available. Be sure your eligible donor is a trusted source to you.

Down Payment

Remember, you can inquire as to how much the percentage down is for each program with your local lender or financial institution. Inquire about each loan program: Federal Housing Administration (FHA), Conventional, United States Department of Agriculture (USDA), Veterans Affairs (VA), etc. Confirm the benefits, pros and cons of each, and do your own research.

As part of your loan process, you may be required to pay a down payment. This down payment is a percentage of the purchase price and depends on the type of mortgage along with other factors. Some loan programs that are backed by the federal government usually do not require down payments (VA loans and USDA loans).

Ex: Let's say if you decided to apply for an FHA loan. The home you selected and are under contract for has a purchase price of $150,000. FHA usually requires as little as 3.5 percent down (to be paid).

To calculate your down payment, you would take your purchase price of $150,000 and multiply it by the percentage down (to be paid), in this case 3.5 percent.

$150,000 x 3.5% = $5,250 would be the amount of the down payment needed.

You may think that this may be a lot of money; however, if you refer to my savings strategies in my *One for the Tenant!* book, it is doable.

If 3 percent is needed for your down payment, go for 5 percent and save that much if you can possibly do it. Take control of your mortgage situation. I personally made a decision to save up not only enough for the down payment but also more to cover any other upfront costs required in the loan (appraisal, closing costs, inspections, etc.).

Some first-time homebuyer programs may offer down payment assistance and grants, but you need to inquire.

Down Payment Assistance

If you are unable to afford your down payment on your own, you may be offered down payment assistance through a qualified program. This is helpful because it pays for your down payment, and it is money you didn't have to save for. While this may all sound very positive, there is a flip side to some of these programs. They may require you to reside in the home for a certain time period, have a specific purchase price limit, higher interest rate, higher closing costs, higher monthly mortgage payment, income limits, etc.

Also, some of the down payment assistance programs are considered "extra assistance loans" and would reflect as a second mortgage lien on your home. There are also certain restrictions as to when this second lien would need to be paid (when you refinance the home, etc.). It is imperative that you try to save as much as you can for your down payment.

One question that helped me in my savings goal was a daily reminder of asking myself, "How bad do you really want your own home?" I made many sacrifices in not purchasing take-out food often or not purchasing items that I wanted but didn't *need.* I gave myself a monthly budget and stuck to it. I also gave myself a deadline for when I wanted to have the funds saved by. In constantly reminding myself that I could do it, I did.

Lender Credit

Some lenders may give lender credits to the borrower to help cover some, part, or all of the closing costs. While it is best to save enough money to cover all of your closing costs, it is good to know that some lenders may offer lender credits.

Remember, if you do receive a lender credit for closing costs, you may be subject to a higher interest rate. Be sure to confirm with your lender. Lender credits are based on what the lender is willing to cover/pay.

Ex: Let's say your closing costs is $7,500 and your lender is willing to offer you a lender credit. The lender decides to pay only $500.00. This is fine because, remember, they can choose to pay how much they want. It is best to work with your financial institution/lender, for not all lenders will offer a lender credit for closing costs but may offer it for something else.

Rates

When applying for a mortgage, everyone opts to obtain the lowest rate possible. The best advice is to shop around and contact different lenders to see what rates they offer. Rates are dependent on different factors including lender credits, down payment assistance, credit, etc. Based on your personal criteria, one lender may offer you a 5 percent rate, while another may offer you a 4.25 percent rate. While it is not much of a difference, it is definitely worth looking into. Whichever lender you decide to choose, be sure you lock in your interest rate. When the lender "locks" your rate, it basically means that whatever the rate is at that current time, they will maintain (hold and use) that rate for a certain time period before you close. Remember, rates fluctuate, so if you believe that you have a good rate, inquire to your loan officer as to how you can lock it in. You can also perform either an online search or contact your lender for current interest rates.

Escrow

When it comes to an escrow account, many people wonder if they should have their lender initiate one or not. This question can be answered by you, but it also will depend on the type of mortgage you are planning to obtain, your lender, and if an escrow account is required or not. Some government-backed programs require an escrow account, so be sure to discuss this with your lender. Hopefully with this explanation, it will help you in your decision.

Simply put, would you like to have the responsibility each month of paying your mortgage payment (principal and interest), hazard insurance, flood insurance (if required), mortgage insurance (if applicable), and property taxes (to name a few) on your own? Or would you like to have your lender establish an escrow account and have your mortgage payment (principal and interest), hazard insurance, flood insurance (if required), mortgage insurance (if applicable), and property taxes, to name a few, deducted each month when they become due? If you decide to have your lender establish an escrow account, remember you are responsible for paying the monthly amount due. Your lender will provide you with monthly payment letters reflecting an amount due depending on the terms of your loan. Be sure you make your monthly payments on time, for the mortgage payment, interest, insurance, taxes, etc. can only be paid if there are funds in the escrow account.

Ex: If your monthly mortgage payment amount (amount reflected on monthly payment letter) is $600.00, you would provide this payment by either direct deposit, mail, or the agreed upon payment method you arranged with the servicer of your loan (your payment letters/stubs will tell you who this is). Once the funds are received by the servicer, it will be placed into your escrow account, and they, in turn, will deduct the mortgage payment, interest, hazard insurance, flood insurance (if required), mortgage insurance (as applicable), property taxes, etc. from this account and pay them as they become due. You will usually receive an escrow statement reflecting payments made, projected balances, taxes, hazard insurance, flood insurance (if required), etc. If you choose to pay these items on your own, please be sure they are paid as they become due. If there are any changes to the property tax amount (increase or decrease), you will be made aware so that you are paying the correct amount. Confirm if there are any extra taxes that a new homeowner needs to pay outside of those that are included in your escrow (some states have fire tax, etc.).

Credit Report/FICO

You can request a free copy of your credit report from the credit bureaus (Equifax, Experian, Transunion). By you requesting a copy of your credit report, it does not affect your FICO score in any way. It provides you with a chance to see what your credit report looks like and work on improving it (bringing accounts current, disputing accounts that are not yours, disputing accounts that reflect the incorrect information, etc.) if needed.

While you are in the mortgage process with one lender, if you decide to switch to another lender for any reason, there is one key item you should know about: hard credit pulls.

Depending on the lender and program, switching to a new lender may require you to start the process from the beginning (new credit pull, new appraisal to be ordered, etc.). You can *sometimes* (based on the loan program criteria) transfer your documents (completed appraisal, home inspections, etc.) from one lender to the other (if the property address is the same).

Remember, there is a certain time frame set from the time the lender first pulls your credit hard pull (all three bureaus with your credit score) to the date of its expiration (this time frame is referenced for the mortgage process only). Once this time has expired, your lender will have to pull your credit again, and your FICO score will be affected and may even decrease. There is no need for concern, for if you continue to pay your monthly debt on time, your score should remain relatively the same. Check with your lender on the amount of time your credit report has from issuance to expiration. You can also request a copy of your credit report from your lender.

If you decide to switch lenders during your mortgage process for whatever reason, be sure you are aware of how many days you have before your credit is pulled again so that your score is not affected.

Ex: You start the mortgage process with lender P, and they complete a hard pull—meaning they pull your credit report with your three FICO scores from all bureaus. Three weeks into the mortgage process, you decide to switch lenders. You contact lender M and advise them that you already had your credit report pulled with lender P. Lender M may not pull your credit report if the time frame has not expired, or they may pull your credit report again depending on program terms and other factors. If lender M does indeed pull your credit report prior to the expiration date (timeframe between when lender P first pulled your credit to the initial expiration date), there should be no major effect to your FICO; however, if it is pulled after the expiration date, there will be some affect. It is imperative for you to confirm this information prior to switching lenders. This way, you are aware of how your credit will be impacted.

Fixing My Credit

Many people are afraid to look at their credit report for fear that it is not sufficient to obtain credit or a home. Take charge of your credit report as with all other aspects of the loan process. Now let's start "fixing" your credit. Once you request a free copy of your credit report (prior to starting the mortgage process) from the credit bureaus, review your report for accuracy. Are all of the accounts on the credit report your accounts? Are the balances accurate? Are the active accounts reflecting the correct creditor (company name)? Check your addresses, employer, social security number, date of birth—are all of those factors accurate? If there are any discrepancies, you can contact the credit bureau and report it for their review.

Next, let's take a look at your FICO score. Is it lower or higher than you expected? If it's higher, great! If it is lower, let's try to improve it. Do you have factors that are bringing it down (late payments, past due amounts, etc.)? Are you able to try and bring these accounts current? If you are unable to make the required payment on the past due account, another option would be to speak to the creditor and work out a payment plan for a lower payment each due date. This will help to pay the debt.

Ex: You have a past due debt on your credit report for furniture store T. You owe furniture store T $3,500 with monthly payments of $150.00. In your current situation, you are not able to pay the monthly payments of $150.00. Instead of continuing to allow this to negatively affect your credit report and reflecting late/past due, you can contact furniture store T and inquire if they can lower the monthly payment on the debt owed. They will do one of many things:

- They can lower it to a manageable monthly payment for you until the debt is paid off (remember, a creditor would rather you pay the amount due in full verses them having to go to a debt collector or other means).
- They can lower your monthly payment for a specific time period and then raise the payment amount to the original terms of the contract.
- They can allow you to select the scheduled payment date that allows you to make your monthly payment on time.
- Etc.

You won't know unless you try. Again, take the reins! You got this!

Credit History

Do you know that you can build your credit history by paying your student loans, auto loans, and other debt on time? Many people think they need many credit cards and a lot of debt to build credit; however, this is the total opposite. The less debt, the better. Be sure you are paying your debt on time and staying consistent on your priorities.

The payment history of an account is a very important factor. The history of an account is usually how long the account has been opened, maintained (current payments, delinquent payments, etc.), and its current standing. Lenders often look for this to determine your ability to pay your mortgage.

Ex: Let's say your credit report reflects three student loans, one auto loan, and one credit card. All of these accounts were opened in 1995. During the time period, you only had one late payment reflected for the credit card, but you have made all payments, bringing the account current. All of the above accounts are actively current. In looking at the history of this situation, you have a longstanding history that these accounts have been active. You have been able to maintain the required payments in a timely fashion. Your FICO scores are also in an excellent range.

Based on these factors, a lender will look and determine if you are able to maintain a longstanding debt such as a mortgage. How well have you been paying your longest standing and other debt, etc.? Have you been applying for a lot of credit in a short period of time? Are your accounts (especially credit cards) close to their limit or maxed out?

In reviewing your credit report, ask yourself this question: How good is your history? If you answer, "Not great," then you know what you need to do to start fixing it. Take it by the reins. You got this! In understanding the above, let's make your credit history a good one.

Remember, it is more about the length of time you have had the debt and how well you have been paying it historically. Do you have a good history in paying your debt? Do you have a bad history of past due/delinquent debt?

As discussed before, there may be extenuating factors that may have caused you to miss making payments on your debt, but once you are able to, try to get back on track.

In looking at my own credit report, I only have two credit cards (that I charge a few items and then pay off by the end of the month) and one mortgage. The longer the credit cards are open builds history. The mortgage adds even more history because it is a longstanding debt, which may take more time to pay off.

Keeping your payments current on the debt you owe will help you to build a good credit history.

Say What?

There are very important terms that you should look out for when reviewing your contract. Below is a brief explanation of two most commonly seen terms.

- A seller may decide to sell and list their home in "as-is" condition. In doing so, this advises the buyer that the seller will not complete any repairs on the home. In this case, you (the buyer) are accepting the home in its "as-is" condition. If there are any major repairs, defects, or issues with the home, you (the buyer) will be responsible for rectifying them. Even though a home is being sold "as-is," the seller still needs to adhere to certain minimum disclosure standards. There may be something wrong or nothing at all wrong with the home. Be sure your contract confirms the specifics regarding the home in the "as-is" sale. You can possibly inquire about the reason they are selling the home in this condition. Your realtor can advise you on what specifically the seller can disclose to you based on your location (state), so try to find a realtor that specializes in this particular market. If you decide that an "as-is" home is best for you, be sure to have a home inspection completed. This way, you will know if there are any defects or issues. Remember, any defects or issues that you discover after you have purchased the home are for you to remedy.

- A seller may decide to sell and list their home "as-is, where-is." This means that the seller is selling the home in its current condition (whatever that may be) and in its current location. The buyer is purchasing home in its "as-is" condition with all of its defects, those known and not known, in its current location—"where-is." It is imperative to confirm any information you possibly can on the current location of the property. Try to obtain information to see what (if anything) is wrong with the current location of the property. To give you some examples of possible "where-is" issues:
  - » "where-is" location being prone to flooding
  - » "where-is" location being prone to earthquakes
  - » "where-is" location being on swampland
  - » "where-is" location is close to wetlands
  - » "where-is" location is next to a cemetery
  - » "where-is" location is prone to pests in yard (snakes, mice, rats, etc.)

Remember, the home is being sold "as-is, where-is" for a reason.

Fixer-Upper vs. Drop Bags Home

The one thing you need to know is that no matter what home you purchase, it will need some form of repair. There is no such thing as a perfect home in condition sense. A seller is always selling a home for a reason. Even though there are property condition disclosures provided from the seller to the buyer (as long as it is not an "as-is" sale where disclosures are not provided), a seller may not disclose all of the issues with the home (though required). It is up to you (the buyer) to complete the necessary required inspections, visual inspections in your initial and final walk-through, and confirm the home is to a suitable standard. Do not rely on the lender, realtor, or broker to determine the condition of the home. A fixer-upper home will need work, but be sure to complete your necessary inspections as needed (mold, lead, pest, etc.). Be sure that you have some funds to handle any possible problems to the home after you have purchased it if needed.

Perform an online search on the address and see if anything interesting pops up.

Home Appraisal

You will not be able to choose the appraiser to complete the appraisal on your home, for the lender does this. Inquire with the lender as to approximately how much the appraisal costs will be for the home. Having the needed funds to pay for your home appraisal prior to closing is required. The appraisal will give you information regarding the home's value, any issues that may need to be addressed, and comps, or comparable properties, to the one that you are purchasing. Finding comps for your home is something you can also perform for your own records. This is usually done by the appraiser when the appraisal report is being completed. If you receive the appraisal and you disagree with the value or comps used, you can provide comps you locate to help support a different (possibly higher) value. When looking for comps, search Zillow or other search engines that can provide you with recently sold homes similar to the one you are purchasing. Be sure to look for similar size, bedrooms, bathrooms, etc. and see how much they sold for. Also check the listing to see if any improvements were done prior to the sale (Ex: new bathroom, kitchen, etc.). Be sure if you are purchasing a condo to look for condos with similar comps, or with single family to look for single family home comps, etc. When the appraiser is selecting a comparable property, they would usually select those within a certain distance to the property you are purchasing or within the same city (subject property) that has been sold recently and shares similar factors to your perspective property (such as the views like streams, lakes, mountains, etc.). This will give you a ballpark area of where your value should range. Review your completed appraisal report in full once received and ask any questions as needed.

Ex: Let's use the scenario below:

- The home you are looking to purchase has an asking price of $160,000.
- The most recent comps all currently sold for $130,000.
- Some questions you would need to ask yourself are:
- Were there any improvements or updates to the home you are purchasing?
- Is the current market warranting a seller's or buyer's?
- Is the seller trying to recoup funds paid on the mortgage (if any)?

If there were no improvements or updates to the home you are purchasing, this may decrease the value of the home when compared to other homes with updates. Usually if this is the case (appraisal value comes in lower than the asking price), the lender would proceed in using the lower of the two values. If the purchase (asking) price is $160,000 and the value of the home is $130,000, the lender would use $130,000. Zillow or another online search engine can help you in giving you a rough estimate as to where the value of the home would reflect.

Let's say your mortgage program has a loan-to-value (LTV) maximum of 90 percent. Once the appraisal is completed, the lender will be able to calculate your LTV amount. This is a calculation that divides the loan amount against the equity (value) in the home you are planning to purchase.

Ex: Your purchase price is $160,000 and the appraisal value from the completed appraisal reflects $190,000.

$$\frac{\$160{,}000 \text{ purchase price}}{\$190{,}000 \text{ appraised value}} = 84.2\% \text{ LTV}$$

With the LTV at 84 percent, this is under the program maximum, so you would qualify.

Home Inspections

You are able to decide which company completes the home inspection for you. Be sure to do your research prior to and look for accredited companies that are reputable. Look at the company reviews and price, contact them for a quote, inquire about scheduling, etc. You will need to have upfront funds to pay for the home inspection on the property. It is usually completed by a certified and trained inspector. They usually perform an inspection of the home and will provide you with a report detailing any noted defects or issues regarding the current condition of the home. If there are any items that need to be remedied, it will reflect on the home inspection. Depending on the severity of the issue or defect on the home; you may have the right to walk away from the transaction, but you will need to check your state laws. Remember that whatever inspection company completes your physical home inspection, other inspections you have requested to be completed you will need to pay for upfront, for these will be borrower costs unless the seller agrees to pay for them. Be sure to contact the company to see how much they charge. Also, once the inspections are completed, obtain a copy of the inspection report. Read it to its entirety, as it will provide you with any possible issues or defects in the property. Since the seller is still the owner, depending on the issue/defect, you both can work together and have them cure (fix) the issue and bring the property up to standard. Once the repairs (if any) are completed by the seller, depending on the severity of the repair, a reinspection may need to be completed, and you will sign off on the repairs (as long as you are satisfied with the repairs done).

You can also choose what other inspections you would like completed on the property. Other inspections include mold, asbestos, lead, foundation, roof, pest (termite), water, and radon, to name a few. You can request these inspections as applicable to the property you are purchasing and your situation.

Remember, you will have to pay for these inspections upfront (prior to them being completed). Just like the initial home inspection, you will be able to choose which company performs the service.

Remember, if you are purchasing a bank-owned home, it is not likely that the bank will cover any repairs needed to the home, especially if the home is being sold "as-is"; you will be responsible for these repairs.

Keep in mind that you should also complete a visual inspection of the property prior to purchasing the home. My two books *One for the Tenant!* and *One for the Landlord!* include sections on specific items along with your own that you should inspect.

Land

You can also decide to purchase land and then build your dream home on it. You will need to apply for a construction loan. There are certain criteria that you will need to know and be aware of prior to proceeding.

- Is there sewer connection available where the home will be located?
- Is electricity available?
- Is there an active water source (city, well, etc.) available?
- Is oil and/or natural gas available?
- Is the land you are planning to purchase buildable (meaning are you able to construct a home on it)?
- Confirm if the land you are purchasing is used for residential purposes.
- Confirm the classification of the property. Is it residential, industrial, commercial, natural resources, agricultural, etc.?
- Is there access to a road from your property?

Lastly, as with a condo and single-family home, you will need to confirm if the land you are planning to purchase and construct your home on is part of an HOA. Yes, it does include land as well! You should be able to contact the HOA to confirm if any fees/dues are outstanding or are paid in full.

Though it may be a bit far-fetched to think of these things, it is worth noting to provide you with a heads up! There are many other factors, but these are important ones to keep in mind when purchasing land to build your home.

Property Boundaries

Now that you are close to purchasing the home or property of your dreams, do you know what parts of the land are yours verses others around you? Knowing where your legal property (boundary) lines, or lot lines, begin and end is very important and can potentially save you any problems or legal matters down the road.

Let's look at two examples:

Example 1: Imagine purchasing a home and deciding to place fencing around the property. You contacted a contractor who completed the fencing around the property as instructed. Another property owner (surrounding your property) has now advised that the fencing you just had installed is partially on their property. Your fencing has now potentially encroached on someone else's boundary line.

Example 2: You decided to purchase a home with beautiful tall trees surrounding the home for privacy reasons. A severe storm passes through the area and some of the trees fall onto the surrounding owner's property. One tree falls on a surrounding owner's shed and another tree falls on another property owner's car, both causing damage. Knowing where your property (boundary) or lot lines are can help determine which property owner is responsible for the trees. If the trees are not within your property line and are legally on the surrounding owner's property line, it will help to determine who is responsible for any potential damage caused by the trees.

To figure out your property lines you can try any of the following resources or others recommended to you:

- Contact your local county recorder or assessor's office.
- Contact a licensed and certified land surveyor to conduct a boundary survey.
- Access public maps of your street and locate your boundaries.

Oil Tank

If you are thinking about purchasing a home that is heated by oil, then there are some things you need to know regarding the oil tank. The first is to confirm if the tank is above or below ground. You may ask, "What is the importance in knowing where the tank is located on the property?" First, some loan programs do not allow for the oil tank to be buried underground. Second, if the tank is indeed underground, when was it last inspected? The tank needs to be inspected to see and determine if there are any leaks, its current condition, etc. An oil tank that is buried underground and is leaking is not environmentally friendly and may have hefty fines associated to the owner if it leaks into the drinking water/ soil. With the tank being above ground it is easier to inspect and confirm what is needed (if anything). All homeowners are different in where the tank is located (underground, basement, above ground, outside the home, etc.). Be sure to confirm with your lender and realtor if purchasing a home with an underground oil tank. The town you are purchasing the home in can also provide you with more information (if needed). It is best to confirm prior to purchasing the home that everything is in compliance. Do not fret, because if the tank is indeed buried underground, the lender can request that the tank be exhumed and inspected.

Cesspool/Septic

Some states have regulations regarding cesspools, especially the installation of them. Some states have actually banned the installation of them. There are also legislations which require that once a home with a cesspool is sold, the new owner (buyer) has within one year to hook up either a septic tank system or connect the home to the city sewer system. All states are different, so be sure to confirm before you purchase a home with a cesspool. Your realtor (as applicable) will be able to advise you if this is the case in your state.

If the home you are purchasing does not have a cesspool, septic, or is not connected to the city sewer, contact your local Department of Public Works. They will be able to confirm if there are indeed sewer connections available for the home (prior to you purchasing it).

It is imperative to confirm that the home you are purchasing has a sewer system.

Flood Insurance

You will also need to search for a homeowner's insurance and flood insurance (if applicable) company. You can do an online search and contact them by telephone. Be sure to have them describe the policy, specific coverages, premiums, costs, etc. in full. If the insurance company offers bundling, inquire as to how much this would cost. Usually, they can provide you with a quote. Obtain the quote or reference number once you have decided on an insurance and provide this to the lender. Flood insurance is a separate policy from homeowner's insurance in that it offers coverage to your home and personal items in the event your home is damaged by flooding. Having a property in close proximity to the water is ideal, but for you as a homeowner, if your property is deemed to be located in a flood zone, you will need to obtain flood insurance coverage on your property. There are also certain circumstances that would *require* you to have flood insurance on your home (i.e., if there is a lien on your property, if your home is in a high-risk flood area, etc.). You can determine if your home is in a flood zone by either reviewing a flood map for your home's location, obtaining a flood certificate (your lender should be able to provide you with one), review the flood zone section on the appraisal, performing an online search to the Federal Emergency Management Agency (FEMA) and searching your home's location, etc. Be sure to discuss in detail with the flood insurance provider of your choice the specifics of the policy and what events are covered (i.e., tsunami, flooding from neighbor's water tank, home is in a high-risk flood area, etc.). Shop around when looking for flood insurance and base your decision on policy contents matching your specific needs, price, deductible, and your personal values.

Homeowner's Insurance

You will also need to search for a homeowner's insurance company. You can do an online search and contact them by telephone. Be sure to have them describe the policy, specific coverages, premiums, costs, etc. in full. If the insurance company offers bundling, inquire as to how much this would cost. Usually, they can provide you with a quote. Obtain the quote or reference number once you have decided on an insurance and provide this to the lender. You need to be sure that you have the sufficient amount of homeowner's insurance coverage for the property you are purchasing. Homeowner's insurance may not be required (depending on your state) but may be mandatory if you have a lien on your home. When contacting an insurance carrier to inquire about the types of homeowner's insurance they provide, be sure the policy and its coverage is explained to you in detail. Remember that all coverages are different, and you would need to cater your policy to your specific needs. Some factors to inquire about (as applicable) to your property are:

- windstorms
- explosions

- sand/dust storms
- fires (wildfires, electrical fires, arson, etc.)
- earthquakes
- hurricanes and other natural disasters (not covered in this list)
- vandalism
- lightning strike
- power failure
- tree falls on home (falling objects)
- damages from your property to another
- damages from another property to yours (in case other owner has no insurance)
- sewage backups

Other items to note is if you suffered a total loss on your home, how much would it cost to rebuild it in its current location? If the property burns down and you are at fault, does your policy cover this event? These are just some factors, and you will need to add any others that are applicable to your property when inquiring about coverage. Discuss the amount of the deductible (if any), for this is the amount you will have to pay before your insurance carrier begins making payments for any covered issues you may experience.

For example: Your homeowner's insurance policy covers damages from wildfires and hurricanes. There was a recent hurricane that passed through the area your home is located in and your home suffered damages to the roof. You contact the insurance carrier to advise them of what happened to the roof on your home. You work closely with the insurance carrier and provide them with any requested items they may need. Before the insurance carrier can begin to make payments for your home repair, you will need to pay your deductible. It is up to you to decide and work closely with the insurance carrier to determine the amount of the deductible that is affordable for you. These are just some factors for you to keep in mind, along with any others that are applicable to your property when inquiring about coverage. Also remember that in the event you sell the property, be sure you cancel the insurance policy. There is no need for you to insure a home you no longer own.

A word of advice for a homeowner who will own a property located in snowy or icy area: Some state laws require the owner to clear the sidewalk in front of their homes so that individuals may pass freely and without hinderance. It is important for you to check your local state laws regarding this matter. If there is heavy snowfall, ice, etc. and someone injures themselves due to you not clearing the sidewalk in front of your residence (if applicable to your area), you could be held liable.

Research your state's laws to determine if the property owner is responsible for clearing the sidewalk during winter storms or if it is the responsibility of the state. Also, if it is the responsibility of the property owner, what are the penalties/fines and how much?

Initial/Final Walk-Through

Congratulations on your upcoming closing! Be sure *prior* to your closing that you confirm with your lender the final amount (if any) that you will need to bring to the closing (down payment, closing costs, etc.). It is imperative *before* you proceed to the closing on your new home to schedule and attend a final walk-through of the property you are purchasing. Be sure to complete the final walk-through as if you are actually residing in the home and determine if the home is in livable condition or not. The home should be in the same condition it was at the time of the initial walk-through (unless agreed upon updates/changes to the home were added in writing to the purchase and sale agreement and completed by the seller/agreed upon party). Also, confirm that all furniture (unless agreements were made in writing in the purchase and sale agreement to remain) has been removed from the home. If furniture is inside or outside against the home during the final walk-through, be sure to check behind and under them (they could be covering potential damages, etc.). The home should be clean, broom swept, free of debris, and in an up to code condition. If permitted, schedule your final walk-through on the same day of the closing (view the property first and then attend the closing). *Do not* allow the home closing to be performed until you have completed the final walk-through. This process is so important that I cannot stress it enough. This will give you one final time to view the property and confirm its condition, before you close and take ownership.

If you discover an issue with the home during the final walk-through, be sure to raise this concern with your attorney, the lender, your agent, and not proceed with the closing until it is resolved. Once you close on the home and accept the deed, absent a few rare situations, you will not have any recourse against the seller.

After Closing

After your closing, you will receive a letter explaining your servicer (company whom you will be making your mortgage payments to) and payment details (including who, where, payment amount, etc.). Your first monthly billing statement includes principal and interest as well as taxes and insurance, etc. (if you decided to escrow).

After closing, contact your city hall or town hall to see if you qualify for any property tax exemptions. If your home will be owner occupied, you may qualify for lower taxes, but check with your state.

Be sure that your new lender has your current physical and mailing address. It would surprise you that the new lender may be still sending mail to your old residence address used during your mortgage process.

If you own a condo, be sure to confirm with the condo board/association who your HOA fee payments are made payable to when they are due, the amount, and the address to mail said payment. Be sure to confirm when the board meetings are held so that you can attend. Since you are an owner of a condo (if you purchased a condo), you should attend the meetings to stay abreast of any changes and all the latest events occurring on the property. You can also voice your thoughts and provide feedback at the meetings. Also be sure to obtain emergency contacts on the board. If you decide to become a memeber of the HOA Board (in some states), the HOA fee is waived and you will no longer pay this fee.

Best Wishes!

There is a lot of information included in this book, and I hope you have received great insight from it. Before you even consider purchasing a home, use these items to give you a starting point. Do your own research prior to getting into the mortgage process.

Your first start should be to determine:

- if you are ready to become a homeowner (financially)
- a budget for your new home (e.g., I will not purchase a home that is worth more than a specific amount.)
- if you have enough funds saved to potentially cover your down payment, inspections (if any), and closing costs (as applicable)
- if you would need to apply for extra assistance (grants, down payment assistance, etc.)
- if there are enough funds saved up after closing to cover any repairs needed to the home and for any unexpected emergencies you may encounter
- if you are willing to say no, negotiate, and ask questions if something does not appear correct in the mortgage process

The subject matter in this book was designed to give you an understanding of becoming a first-time homebuyer and important factors to keep in mind. The material in this book in no way should be substituted for legal or financial advice. Try as best as you can to save for your down payment and closing costs (if possible). Be sure you conduct an initial and final walk-through of the property. Remember to save, no matter how small the amount you put aside each time. If possible, please try the example given in the "savings" section of my *One for the Tenant!* book. It will surprise you that you can accomplish it. Remember, there is usually some wiggle room in the different situations you will encounter during your home purchasing journey, so do not be afraid to ask. Remember you got this!

About the Author

A little about me . . . I was born and raised in the beautiful United States Virgin Islands. I have worked in the mortgage compliance industry for over seventeen years, the last two as a Regulatory Analyst and Advisor. I am also certified as a Certified Financial Coach Professional (CFCP) and a Master Certified Professional Coach (MCPC). Throughout my entire mortgage compliance career, I have come to understand that there is such a tremendous need for simplified educational materials, as reflected in this book, for first-time home buyers or anyone planning to own a home. I felt that it was my obligation to help educate anyone planning to purchase a home or property by providing them with the information they may not have known or have heard of in an easy-to-understand way. My hopes to all of my readers is that you use the insights provided in this book to take the reins on your purchase. Go into your potential purchase with knowledge and understanding, remembering to never be afraid to ask questions or question something that does not look right. Always trust your gut!

To my readers, thank you for stopping by, and I wish you many blessings always on your journey!

See you on the upcoming read!

Coming Soon . . .
By J. Baptiste

One for the Landlord!
One for the Tenant!